DEBUGGING LIFE: HILARIOUS MISADVENTURES FROM THE IT TRENCHES

Inside the Wild World of IT:

Memes, Mishaps, and Mayhem

WEENDZOR LOUIME

Contents

CHAPTER ONE

Welcome to the Tech Circus

The IT Department: A Carnival of Characters

In the bustling ecosystem of the IT department, each character is a colorful thread woven into the fabric of tech hilarity. Take Dave, the eternal optimist and self-proclaimed "network ninja," who believes every connectivity issue can be solved with a clever pun and a few well-placed memes. One day, when the entire the office was plunged into darkness due to a power outage; Dave strolled in with a flashlight and a grin, declaring, "Looks like we're on a power-saving plan! Who's up for some 'light' coding?" His attempts to lighten the situation fell flat, much like the Wi-Fi signal during lunch hours. Yet, his relentless positivity kept the team's spirits high, even if their connectivity was low.

Then there's Linda, the queen of the office pranks, who treats the IT department like her personal playground. She once replaced all the keyboard keys with upside-down versions, leading to a day filled with typos and bewildered faces. "I just wanted to see who could still type without looking!" she cackled as chaos ensued. Her pièce de résistance was when she swapped out the coffee in the break room with decaf, claiming it was a "low-caffeine productivity boost." The caffeine withdrawal led to a full-scale revolt, complete with signs reading "We Want Real Coffee!" Meanwhile, Linda just sipped her decaf and giggled in the corner, fully aware of the havoc she had unleashed.

Tech support calls are another treasure trove of hilarity, especially when you encounter Steve, the "help desk guru." Armed with a headset and a sarcastic wit sharper than any blade, he handles calls with the finesse of a stand-up comedian. One unforgettable call involved a user convinced her computer had a ghost because it kept "talking back" whenever they typed. "Ma'am, that's just the speech-to-text feature," Steve replied, stifling laughter. "Unless the ghost tries to email you, we're in the clear." This knack for humor diffuses tension and makes even the most panicked users chuckle, ensuring they leave the call with a smile—if not a solution.

Amidst the chaos, the IT conference fails are tales to behold, especially when the team decides to present their new software tool. Picture the scene: a projection screen that inexplicably shuts down mid-presentation, leaving everyone staring at a blank wall. Instead of panicking, Mark, the resident "techie," turned to the audience and said, "Well, this is our new software—completely invisible and utterly user-friendly!" The laughter that erupted made the technical hiccup almost a highlight of the event, proving that sometimes the best presentations come from a place of spontaneity and humor rather than perfection.

Lastly, the trials of remote work have birthed their own brand of comedy in the department. With video calls turning into accidental showcases of everyone's living rooms, it's hard to forget the infamous "cat on the keyboard" incident. During a serious project meeting, Tim's feline companion decided to make a cameo by walking across his keyboard, typing out a string of random characters that left everyone in stitches. "I didn't know we had a new team member! Welcome to the project, Mr. Whiskers!" his colleagues joked. This blend of tech and personal life perfectly illustrates how the IT department thrives on humor, making even the most mundane tasks feel like a carnival of characters, each bringing their flair to the chaotic world of technology.

Juggling Code and Coffee: A Day in the Life

The day begins with the familiar sound of the alarm clock blaring, often accompanied by the realization that the coffee supply is dangerously low. As an IT professional, the quest for caffeine is akin to debugging a complex code—frustrating and essential. The morning routine resembles a chaotic sprint, with the coffee machine sputtering like an outdated server while the toaster burns the bagel to a crisp. By the time the first sip of coffee hits the lips, there's a 50/50 chance of it being either a delightful jolt or a burnt disaster that could rival a failed server crash. This is when sanity is restored, and the day is set in motion, albeit with a caffeine-fueled gamble.

Arriving at the office, the first task is often to engage in the daily ritual of greeting coworkers, which typically involves a mix of awkward nods and the occasional attempt at small talk. Most conversations revolve around the latest tech memes circulated in the team chat, leading to a heated debate over which one accurately reflects the never-ending struggle of updating software on a Friday afternoon. The office banter quickly escalates into an impromptu meme competition, where the winner earns the coveted title of "Meme Master" until the next hilarious disaster strikes. Of course, the real prize is the laughter that echoes through the cubicles, drowning out the quiet hum of servers and the frantic clattering of keyboards.

As the workday unfolds, it's time to tackle the coding

assignments, which often come with their own comedic twists. Imagine coding a feature that's supposed to streamline the user experience, only to accidentally create a new button that performs a completely random function, like ordering pizza or triggering a dance party in the office. The ensuing chaos is a sight to behold, with colleagues scrambling to figure out how to turn off the disco lights while simultaneously explaining to the boss why their productivity has suddenly plummeted. These moments serve as a reminder that in the world of IT, the line between genius and absurdity is remarkably thin.

Lunch breaks are usually a mixture of refueling and strategizing the next great office prank. Picture a group of tech-savvy individuals plotting to swap out the coffee with decaf and watching the chaos unfold as their caffeine-dependent colleagues slowly realize something is off. The reactions range from confusion to outright panic, with one colleague dramatically clutching their empty mug like a life preserver in a sea of despair. During these times, the true spirit of camaraderie shines through as everyone bonds over their shared love for pranks, coding mishaps, and the occasional tech support horror story.

As the day winds down, the IT team gathers for their weekly meeting, where the agenda is often a thinly veiled excuse for a comedy show. With each member sharing their funniest tech support call or the latest remote work fail, the atmosphere shifts from mundane to hilarious in mere moments. One story involves a user who couldn't figure out why their computer wouldn't turn on, only to discover they had been trying to boot up a monitor without plugging it in. Laughter erupts, and the meeting turns into a roast of epic proportions, reminding everyone that amidst the juggling of code and coffee, the humor in everyday mishaps truly keeps the IT world spinning.

CHAPTER TWO

Hilarious Tech Support Calls

"Have You Tried Turning It Off and On Again?"

In IT, "Have you tried turning it off and on again?" has become the universal mantra of tech support, akin to a Jedi's lightsaber: seemingly simple but potent. Picture this: a frantic user calls in, their voice quaking like an amateur actor in a horror film. "My computer isn't working!" they wail. You can practically hear the mental gears grinding as you respond, "Have you tried turning it off and on again?" This is the moment when every IT professional knows they're either about to embark on a heroic rescue mission or stumble into a punchline that will haunt them for years.

Remember one Friday afternoon when the entire office was chaotic because Karen from accounting couldn't access the financial software? The whole team gathered around her desk like it was the main stage of a circus, and the only act was a spinning wheel of doom. You were met with wide-eyed disbelief as you calmly suggested the age-old solution. "You can't be serious!" she exclaimed, clutching her coffee like a life raft. After some coaxing, she reluctantly hit the power button. Lo and behold, the program sprang back to life, and you were hailed as the office hero—until the following Monday when she claimed you'd just gotten lucky and that she "totally knew" something was wrong with her computer.

Then there's the classic tale of the remote work debacle. One of your colleagues, let's call him Dave, was working from home when his video conferencing app decided to stage a protest. With a face that could launch a thousand memes, Dave spent fifteen minutes trying to convince his laptop that it was not, in fact, an inanimate object with a vendetta against him. After a series of frantic keyboard smashes and an inspirational speech about the importance of teamwork, he finally succumbed to the inevitable: a forceful power cycle. And just like that, the connection was restored. The moment his camera flickered back on, he was greeted not by applause but by a chorus of laughter as his cat, apparently a tech support expert, sauntered across the keyboard, having orchestrated the entire fiasco.

On the conference circuit, the phrase has taken on a life of its own. At a recent IT expo, a speaker was showcasing the latest cloud technology when his presentation tool froze mid-slide, leaving the audience staring at a lovely image of a beach sunset. In a bold move, he grinned and said, "Well, folks, have you tried turning it off and on again?" The crowd erupted in laughter, and suddenly the entire room was filled with stories of tech fails and heroic recoveries. The poor guy turned a glitch into a comedy routine, proving yet again that IT professionals are the true masters of improvisation—especially when salvaging a tech disaster with a well-timed joke.

As we navigate the wild world of IT, we learn that sometimes the simplest solutions yield the greatest laughter. The next time a colleague looks like they're about to throw their device out the window, just remember the power of that one simple phrase. It's not just a solution; it's a badge of honor, a shared joke among professionals. So the next time you hear someone exclaim, "My computer is dead!" you can confidently lean back in your chair and say, "Have you tried turning it off and on again?" After all, it's not just about fixing problems; it's about embracing the hilarity that comes with the territory.

The 10 Most Outrageous User Requests

In the chaotic world of IT, user requests can sometimes seem like they've been pulled straight from a sitcom script. Picture this: a user walks in, looking like they just survived a tornado, clutching their laptop like a lifeboat. "My computer is making a weird noise!" they exclaim, eyes wide with panic. When you take a moment to listen closely, it sounds suspiciously like a cat purring. Turns out it's just a harmless fan, but in their mind, they're already crafting a horror story about a haunted laptop. This is just one of the many outrageous requests that make IT professionals wonder if they've inadvertently signed up for a reality TV show.

Then there's the classic "Can you make my computer go faster?" This request often accompanies an equally baffling follow-up: "Can you also make it waterproof?" Apparently, some users believe that IT possesses magical powers capable of defying the laws of physics and technology. They seem to forget that we're not wizards; we can't just wave a wand and conjure up a brand-new gaming rig. We can only suggest they stop downloading every "must-have" software that promises to make their computer "run like new" while secretly turning it into a digital graveyard.

We can't forget the infamous "I spilled coffee on my keyboard" debacle. This request usually accompanies a frantic, caffeine-fueled confession that they "might have added too much cream." The keyboard, which now resembles a sticky science experiment, is a testament to the user's commitment to multitasking. When asked if they tried to dry it off, the response is often a sheepish grin and an admission that they "thought it would be fine." In these moments, IT professionals must channel their inner zen masters, reminding themselves that coffee is a food group, even if it's now residing in USB ports.

Then there's the unforgettable "Can you fix my printer?" saga, which often spirals into a comedy of errors. Users can entangle the printer in a web of cables that would make a tech-savvy spider proud. The pièce de résistance is when they dramatically declare, "But it was working just fine yesterday!" as if the printer has a personal vendetta against them. After a thorough investigation, it's revealed that the printer has been out of ink for two weeks, and they had been blissfully ignoring the blinking warning light. At this point, IT professionals often consider getting a "printer whisperer" certification just to deal with these situations.

Lastly, let's not overlook the tech support calls defying logic. A classic example includes a user who, in an effort to increase productivity, decided to "reinvent" their workflow by dragging their entire desktop into the recycling bin. When asked how they planned to retrieve their files, the response was a confused stare, as if the concept of digital trash had never crossed their mind. These moments not only test the patience of IT professionals but also serve as a reminder that the line between comedy and tragedy is often blurred in the realm of user requests. Each outrageous request adds to the rich tapestry of IT life, ensuring that the laughter never fades in the trenches.

CHAPTER THREE

Misadventures in Coding

The Day I Accidentally Deleted the Server

It was a typical Tuesday in the IT department, which meant the coffee pot was running low, the printer was mysteriously jammed, and the smell of burnt toast wafted in from the break room—an unholy combination of tech and culinary disaster. As I sat at my desk pondering the mysteries of life, like why the intern still thought "Ctrl+Z" would undo his bad haircut, I received an email that would change my day forever. It was a routine maintenance reminder from our server admin, a friendly nudge to update the software. Little did I know that that reminder would send me spiraling into a digital Bermuda Triangle.

In my classic overzealousness, I decided to take matters into my own hands. With the arrogance only a caffeinated IT professional can muster, I dove into the server settings like a kid in a ball pit, blissfully unaware of the impending doom. I clicked and clacked away, humming my favorite tune, which coincidentally was the theme song from 'The IT Crowd.' Oh, the irony! When I realized something was terribly off, I had already hit the delete button with the finesse of a drunk elephant at a ballet recital. In that split second, I knew I had committed a cardinal sin of IT—the kind that would make even the most seasoned techies weep.

Panic set in faster than a Windows update on a Monday morning. My heart raced as I frantically searched for the "Undo" option, but it was nowhere to be found. I could almost hear the server laughing at me, mocking my ignorance as I imagined all the data swirling down the digital drain. My colleagues, blissfully unaware, continued their mundane tasks, blissfully ignorant that their lives were about to be turned upside down by my epic blunder. I envisioned an apocalyptic scenario where I would have to explain to the boss why our entire database had just become a digital ghost town, complete with tumbleweeds and eerie silence.

As I braced myself to break the news, I felt a strange mix of dread and curiosity. What would the fallout be? Would I be the subject of office memes for eternity? Would I be forced to wear an "I Deleted the Server" T-shirt at the next IT conference? My fears were confirmed when I finally confessed to my team. Instead of pitchforks and torches, I was met with laughter. It turned out that they had all experienced similar mishaps, and my blunder was just another chapter in the never-ending saga of tech shenanigans that had bonded us all. At that moment, I realized I wasn't just an IT professional but part of a fraternity of digital misfits who wore our mistakes like badges of honor.

In the aftermath, we rallied together to restore the server, sharing stories of our own tech catastrophes while simultaneously setting up a "Server Protection Fund" to keep my delete-happy fingers at bay. We even organized a 'Delete Day' where we could safely vent our frustrations through harmless office pranks—such as switching the keyboard layouts or hiding the coffee. As we laughed and shared our tales, it became clear that humor is the best debugging tool in the IT world. So the next time you find yourself on the brink of deleting something important, remember: it's not the server at risk; your reputation may need a little humor to survive.

Debugging: My Personal Horror Stories

Debugging can often feel like a scene from a horror movie, complete with unexpected jumpscares and plot twists that leave you questioning your sanity. I remember one particular night when I was the lone warrior in the trenches of a critical project. As I stared into the abyss of my code, I made the grave mistake of deciding to add a feature at 2 AM. I didn't realize I had just opened Pandora's box. When I hit compile, my screen erupted like a volcano, spewing errors that seemed to mock me. I swear the error messages laughed as if they had conspired against me. The only thing missing was a creepy soundtrack and a chatty ghost urging me to give up.

One of my colleagues, let's call him Dave, has a horror story involving an innocent line of code and a very active alert system. During a high-stakes demonstration to potential clients, Dave decided to showcase a new feature that would notify users of system updates. He didn't know that a simple misconfiguration would trigger a cascade of notifications every two seconds. The poor clients were bombarded with alerts that read, "Update available! Update available! Update available!" It turned into a bizarre techno-rave meets corporate pitch. Dave's face turned from confident to ghostly pale, and I could almost hear him thinking, "I should've just stuck to my day job of making coffee."

Then there was the time I attempted to impress a date with my coding skills. I thought I'd show off my latest project, a sleek app designed to simplify daily tasks. The romantic ambiance was set, and I felt like a tech-savvy Casanova. However, when I launched the app, it crashed spectacularly, leaving my date staring at my screen as if it had revealed my deepest, darkest secrets. There I was, scrambling to debug in real time while maintaining a semblance of charm. The irony was not lost on me; I had just turned a potential love story into a tragic comedy, complete with awkward silence and the sound of my self-esteem hitting rock bottom.

Remote work has its own unique flavor of debugging horror. My team decided to host a virtual meeting to discuss our latest project, and I was tasked with presenting. Everything was going smoothly until my cat, who apparently had a vendetta against my professional life, jumped onto my keyboard mid-presentation. The screen has random characters and a delightful mix of cat memes. My coworkers erupted in laughter, and I felt my dignity slipping through my fingers like a poorly written script. I tried to regain control, but the cat was already winning the hearts of everyone on the call. If only I had thought to hire him as my co-presenter; he certainly had better comedic timing than I did.

Finally, let me regale you with the tale of our annual IT conference, where pranks and shenanigans are as common as free Wi-Fi. One year, a group of us decided to prank the keynote speaker, who was notorious for his overly serious demeanor. We replaced his slides with hilarious memes that depicted him as a tech superhero battling "The Bug" in various ridiculous scenarios. As he stepped on stage, his expression shifted from confusion to horror, and the audience was in stitches. It was a glorious moment of collective laughter until we realized he had a knack for improvisation. He turned the tables, incorporating the memes into his presentation and our prank into a conference highlight. In the end, we learned that sometimes, the biggest horror stories can lead to the biggest laughs, reminding us that humor is often the best debugging tool in IT.

CHAPTER FOUR

Office Pranks and Tech Shenanigans

The Great Keyboard Swap

In the heart of a bustling IT department, where the hum of servers and the click-clack of keyboards created a symphony of productivity, a prank was brewing that would go down in the annals of office legend. It all began when Tim, the resident jokester and self-proclaimed "King of the IT Prank Wars," decided it was high time to inject some hilarity into the mundane routine of coding and troubleshooting. His target? The unsuspecting, perpetually serious Bob was known for his laser focus on his work and his uncanny ability to fix any bug in record time. Tim knew Bob wouldn't see the prank coming, and that was part of the fun.

The plan was simple yet diabolically effective: Tim would execute "The Great Keyboard Swap." Armed with a collection of spare keyboards, he stealthily replaced Bob's beloved mechanical keyboard with one that looked almost identical but had the keys rearranged in a nonsensical order. As he completed the swap, Tim could barely contain his laughter, imagining the confused look on Bob's face when he returned to his desk. He was unaware that the ensuing chaos would exceed his most ambitious expectations.

When Bob returned, he sat down, fingers poised to attack a particularly tricky piece of code. A cacophony of miskeyed commands followed, turning his usually rapid-fire typing into a slow-motion train wreck. Every time he intended to type "if," he ended up with "wg." His attempts to compile left him staring at error messages that might as well have been in hieroglyphics. The rest of the team, monitoring the situation from their desks, erupted in laughter as they watched Bob's baffled expression morph into a mounting frustration. It was a sight to behold, like watching a cat trying to catch a laser pointer.

As Bob's confusion escalated, so did the hilarity. He started pacing back and forth, muttering like a mad scientist on the brink of a breakthrough. "Why is my code possessed?" he exclaimed, slamming his fist on the desk. "Is this some kind of sick joke?" Unable to contain himself, Tim finally stepped in to reveal the prank. Bob, initially taken aback, couldn't help but crack a smile. Sure, his productivity had taken a nosedive, but the absurdity was too rich to ignore. They all agreed that this was the best laugh the department had had in months.

In the aftermath of "The Great Keyboard Swap," a new tradition was born. Tim was crowned the prankster of the year, and the team decided to incorporate humor into their daily grind. They even created a 'Prank of the Month' club, where each member would take turns pulling mild, harmless pranks on one another, ensuring that the spirit of camaraderie and laughter remained alive. Bob, of course, became the vigilant guardian of his keyboard, implementing a series of increasingly elaborate security measures that included password-protected keyboard covers and a suspicious eye on anyone approaching his desk. Ultimately, they all learned that a little laughter in the IT trenches goes a long way in keeping the morale high amidst the never-ending cycle of debugging and coding.

The Chair That Went Rogue

A chair that had seen better days sat in a quiet corner of the office, nestled between the server room and the coffee machine. The chair creaked at the slightest movement, a relic from when ergonomic design was merely a suggestion. Little did anyone know, this chair aspired far beyond supporting weary techies during long coding sessions. One fateful Monday morning, the chair decided it was time to assert its independence as the team gathered for their usual stand-up meeting. With a dramatic squeak and a rebellious lurch, it rolled itself right out of the conference room, leaving the IT team in a state of bewildered laughter.

As the chair made its grand escape, the team couldn't help but giggle at the absurdity of the moment. It was as if the chair had watched too many sci-fi movies and decided to take matters into its own... legs? The office soon transformed into a chaotic scene reminiscent of a live-action cartoon. Colleagues leaped from their seats, chasing after the rogue chair as it darted down the hallway. The chair zigzagged between desks, dodging unsuspecting coworkers who were blissfully unaware of the impending chaos. Emails went unanswered, code went uncompiled, and the great chair chase became the day's highlight.

In the midst of the pandemonium, our fearless IT manager, Dave, decided to act. Armed with a makeshift lasso from a spare Ethernet cable, he proclaimed, "I will bring this chair back to the fold!" What ensued was a series of slapstick attempts to corral the rebellious seat. The chair, however, seemed to possess an uncanny ability to evade capture, expertly maneuvering around corners and occasionally reversing course. It was a race against time, with colleagues cheering on the sidelines, tossing suggestions like, "Maybe it just needs a software update!" and "Have you tried turning it off and on again?"

As the chase wore on, the chair finally reached its final destination: the break room where a group of employees were blissfully enjoying their lunch. With a final, triumphant roll, it wedged itself neatly between the fridge and the microwave as if claiming its throne. Laughter erupted as the team gathered around, marveling at the audacity of the chair. Dave, panting and defeated, could only shake his head in disbelief. "I guess it's a case of 'if you can't beat them, join them,'" he joked as they all settled in for an impromptu lunch meeting, the chair still stubbornly refusing to return to its rightful place.

The legend of the chair that went rogue quickly spread throughout the office. It became an inside joke, sparking a wave of office pranks that involved decorating the chair with sticky notes and Post-its proclaiming its newfound freedom. Team members began leaving snacks for the chair, convinced it had developed a personality. Those who dared to sit in it were met with exaggerated gasps and mock warnings about the "rebellious spirit" that dwelled within. In the end, the chair was retired to a corner of the office as a trophy, a reminder that even the most mundane objects can bring a little laughter into the often monotonous world of IT.

CHAPTER FIVE

IT Conference Fails

Keynote Gone Wrong

Picture this: it's the annual IT conference, and the keynote speaker is a rock star in the tech world, known for her groundbreaking work in machine learning. The room is packed with eager professionals, many of whom have traveled halfway across the country just to hear her insights. As she strides confidently onto the stage, the audience buzzes with excitement. But then, in a twist worthy of a sitcom, she trips over the mic cord and face-plants right onto the stage. The silence is palpable, followed by a wave of suppressed laughter that ripples through the crowd. We're unsure if we're there to learn or witness a physical comedy show.

After a few awkward moments, she scrambles to her feet, brushing off her blazer like a true pro. "I meant to do that," she quips, and the crowd laughs. But the mishaps don't stop there. As she begins her presentation, the projector decides it's a perfect time to stage a rebellion. Instead of her meticulously prepared slides, the audience is treated to a random collection of cat memes and GIFs. One particularly cheeky feline, wearing glasses, stares intently at the screen, mocking the concept of "serious business." The speaker, undeterred, leans into the chaos and starts explaining how AI could potentially help in "understanding the emotional complexities of cats."

When we think it couldn't get any worse, the speaker's laptop freezes mid-presentation, displaying the dreaded spinning wheel of doom. A brave soul from the audience shouts, "Have you tried turning it off and on again?" The crowd laughs, and our fearless speaker, taking a page from the IT playbook, acknowledges the suggestion. She points to her laptop and jokingly asks, "Is this the part where we all collectively chant 'reboot'?" It's a moment of camaraderie that unites the room, reminding everyone that we're all dealing with our versions of tech nightmares at the end of the day.

The climax of this keynote gone wrong comes when she decides to embrace the chaos. She improvises, creating a game where audience members can submit their tech fails via social media. The hashtag #KeynoteFails trends within minutes, and soon, stories about forgotten passwords, accidental replies-all, and rogue printer jams flood in. What started as a disastrous keynote transforms into a hilarious and relatable moment, connecting IT professionals in a way that dry statistics never could. The laughter is infectious; suddenly, the conference feels less like a series of lectures and more like a gathering of friends swapping war stories.

As the event wraps up, the speaker leaves the stage with a triumphant grin, turning a potential disaster into an unforgettable experience. Her expertise and ability to adapt and find humor in the chaos inspires the audience. As we all file out, the buzz is not about the latest technological advancements but rather the shared experience of an epic keynote that has gone wrong. In the world of IT, where glitches and gaffes are an everyday occurrence, it's a reminder that sometimes, the best learning happens when things don't go according to plan – and laughter is the best debugging tool of all.

Networking Nightmares

Picture this: it's a typical Friday evening, and the IT department has organized a networking event to foster camaraderie and knowledge sharing among the team and other departments. The IT manager proudly starts the presentation as the lights dim and the projector warms up. The first slide reads, "Networking: Connecting People and Ideas." As he hits the next button, the projector flickers and displays a cat meme instead. Cue laughter and confusion. The IT manager had forgotten to close his meme folder, leaving the audience to witness a cascading gallery of animals, each more ridiculous than the last. Nothing says professional networking like a cat wearing sunglasses and a Hawaiian shirt.

As the evening progresses, the team engages in light-hearted icebreakers. They split into groups for a game of "Tech Pictionary." One brave soul, armed with a whiteboard marker, begins to draw what he believes is a router but instead ends up with a scribbled interpretation resembling a mix between a toaster and an alien spaceship. The teams debate fiercely, with one group insisting it's clearly "a failed attempt at homebrewing Wi-Fi," while another swears it's "just an angry piece of hardware." By the end of the game, nobody had gained any insights into networking, but everyone had amassed a collection of terrible drawings that would haunt their Slack channels for months to come.

The night's highlight arrives when someone suggests a "Tech Support Call Improv" session. Volunteers are ready to reenact the most outrageous tech support calls they've ever experienced. One IT professional impersonates a user who calls in, convinced that their computer is haunted because the cursor keeps moving on its own. The twist? It's just the user's cat walking across the keyboard. The audience roars with laughter as the impromptu actor channels a mix of confusion and utter disbelief, prompting an imaginary ghost to "explain" why it prefers to play Minesweeper over actual work.

As the networking event nears its end, the team decides to document their evening with selfies, but it becomes a comedy of errors. With a penchant for dramatic angles, the designated photographer captures photos that make everyone look like unflattering caricatures or accidental horror movie stars. The best shot? A group of colleagues attempting to show off their "serious IT faces," but one coworker is caught mid-sneeze, resulting in a snapshot that should undoubtedly be framed and hung in the break room—right next to the "Most Likely to Break the Internet" award.

When they think the night cannot get any more chaotic, the Wi-Fi goes down, leading to a collective gasp. Instead of panic. However, the team laughs, realizing they've turned a networking event into a nightmare. They huddle around their mobile hotspots, sharing their best stories about the struggles of remote work and the trials of video calls gone wrong. Who knew that a night meant for a connection could end with so much laughter and chaos? As they clean up, they agree to make this an annual tradition—because nothing builds teamwork quite like shared disasters and a mutual love for cat memes.

CHAPTER SIX

Geeky Dating Disasters

The Date with a Firewall

It was a typical Tuesday in the IT department when Dave decided to mix things up with a little "firewall date." Dave had recently broken up with his girlfriend, and rather than sulk over a pint of ice cream, he thought it would be a great idea to invite a firewall to dinner. Not just any firewall, mind you, but the company's shiny new next-gen firewall that had been the talk of the break room for weeks. As he set up the "date," he envisioned a romantic evening filled with data packets and encrypted conversations. Little did he know, this date would quickly go off the rails.

When Dave arrived at the server room, he pulled out a candle (which was actually a USB-powered light) and set it next to the firewall. He had even printed a menu of network protocols, intending to impress his digital date with his TCP/IP layers knowledge. As he poured a glass of his finest office water, Dave confidently declared, "Tonight, we're going to do a deep packet inspection of love." Unfortunately, his grand plans were about to be derailed by an unexpected visitor: Janet from HR, who walked in just as he was about to toast to "firewall security."

Janet stood in the doorway, arms crossed, looking as if she had just witnessed a cat video gone wrong. "Is this a date or are you trying to get fired?" she quipped, eyeing the firewall with disbelief and amusement. Dave, ever the quick thinker, replied, "I'm just conducting a security assessment of my heart." With that, he attempted to woo her with his best IT puns, but all he got in return was a smirk and a suggestion to "keep the romance out of the server room." Clearly, his firewall date was losing its spark, and the only thing getting fired was his dignity.

Determined to salvage the evening, Dave introduced some "spontaneity" into the mix. He pulled up a live traffic monitor on the screen, hoping it would inspire playful banter. "Look at all this data flowing in," he said, "just like my hopes for a second date." Now chuckling, Janet said, "Careful, Dave, you might get flagged for inappropriate behavior." At this point, the firewall seemed more interested in blocking Dave's attempts at romance than facilitating any connection. Instead of a love story, they created a hilarious tech support call that no one would ever forget.

As the banter continued, the firewall decided to chime in with its own "input." Suddenly, the alarm went off, signaling a potential breach—unbeknownst to Dave, he had accidentally triggered a false alarm while trying to impress Janet with his "networking skills." The lights flickered, and the server room filled with the sound of beeping alarms, turning what was supposed to be a romantic evening into a chaotic scene reminiscent of an IT conference fail. Dave's romantic aspirations were officially toast, along with any hope of a date with Janet, who was now doubled over in laughter as she watched him scramble to reset the system.

In the aftermath, Dave's disastrous firewall date became a legendary story in the IT department. It was retold in meetings, transformed into memes, and even inspired an office prank where colleagues began inviting various hardware components to "dates" to see what would happen. While Dave may not have found love that evening, he did discover something far more valuable: the understanding that sometimes, in the world of IT, the best connections happen when you least expect them—even if they involve firewalls, alarms, and a healthy dose of laughter.

Love in the Time of Bitrates

In the digital age, where love can be as pixelated as a low-resolution GIF, navigating romantic relationships often feels like troubleshooting a stubborn network connection. Picture it: two IT professionals trying to schedule a date. One suggests a time, but the other's calendar software crashes. They settle on a compromise, only to find that one has accidentally double-booked with a mandatory Zoom meeting about cybersecurity protocols. It's a classic case of "love in the time of bitrates"—where every romantic gesture is fraught with the risk of miscommunication and bandwidth limitations.

As if dating in the tech world isn't complicated enough, there's a new level of hilarity when you throw in office pranks. Imagine one partner surprises the other with a romantic dinner, candles, and a fancy playlist. Instead, they inadvertently stream a conference call for the entire IT department. Suddenly, romantic music is replaced by a heated debate over the merits of cloud storage versus local servers, and the mood shifts from romantic to awkward faster than you can say "buffering." It's a reminder that even the most well-intentioned plans can go hilariously awry in the tech realm.

Tech support calls also have their unique charm when love is involved. Consider a couple who met while debugging a particularly stubborn piece of code. They decide to relive their first encounter by calling tech support together for a glitch in their home network. Instead of a smooth interaction, they are in a comedic spiral of escalating issues. The tech support representative, oblivious to their romantic backstory, starts asking them to reset their modem—while they're in a passionate debate about whose fault it was that the Wi-Fi went down during a critical moment of their favorite show. Love and tech support, it seems, are a recipe for pure comedy.

Remote work has added another layer of absurdity to the romantic lives of IT professionals. Picture a couple attempting a virtual date night over a video call. In a moment of forgetfulness, one partner decides to share their screen to show off a recipe, only to inadvertently reveal their desktop with memes of cats coding and an embarrassing collection of failed programming projects. The other person can't help but burst out laughing, and suddenly, what was meant to be a romantic evening turns into a roast of each other's digital mishaps. These moments of vulnerability remind us that love, like technology, often requires a sense of humor to survive the glitches.

Ultimately, navigating love in the tech world is a series of hilarious misadventures, each with its own debugging challenges. From awkward office interactions to tech conference fails that leave you questioning your dating choices, the journey is anything but smooth. It's a reminder that whether you're submitting a bug report or a heart emoji, laughter is the best patch to any romantic software. So, while we may be coding in the language of love, let's not forget to debug the laughs along the way.

CHAPTER SEVEN

Office Memes Come to Life

When the "This Is Fine" Meme Became Reality"

In IT, the "This Is Fine" meme became an unofficial mascot for the daily chaos we often face. Picture this: deep in the code trenches, a developer notices an error message that seems to multiply like rabbits in spring. Instead of panic, he leans back in his chair, sips his lukewarm coffee, and mutters, "This is fine," as the error logs overflow. It's a scene that would make even the most seasoned techie chuckle at the absurdity of it all. We've all been there, right? That moment when everything is on fire, and you're just hoping that the fire extinguisher is within reach—or at least you have a database backup.

As deadlines loom and pressure mounts, the line between humor and despair blurs. Take the time when a team decides to roll out a new software update without properly testing it. On the launch day, the screens turned into a digital hellscape, flashing error messages like they were trying to communicate with aliens. Instead of panicking, the team gathered in the conference room, coffee in hand, and shared stories of past tech catastrophes, all while the system continued to crumble outside. It was a surreal moment, where laughter became the only coping mechanism left, proving that sometimes the best way to deal with impending doom is to embrace it with a grin.

Remote work has only amplified this phenomenon. Imagine a Zoom meeting where the entire team is discussing a critical issue. Still, in the background, one colleague's cat decides it's the perfect time to walk across the keyboard, triggering a cascade of notifications and alerts. While the team attempts to remain professional, the cat's antics are met with a chorus of laughter and the realization that this is indeed fine. The absurdity of it all serves as a reminder that in the realm of tech, chaos is just a part of the job description. Who needs a stress ball when you have a feline coworker providing comic relief?

Office pranks have taken on a life of their own in this reality. One IT department decided to tape a giant "This Is Fine" meme over the server room door, just as a lighthearted jab at the constant issues that seemed to arise. The first time the new intern walked in, he paused, read the sign, and burst into laughter. Instead of feeling overwhelmed by the day's crisis, he was reminded that sometimes the best response to a meltdown is embracing its ridiculousness. These little moments create bonds among colleagues and turn stressful days into shared memories filled with laughter.

Ultimately, the "This Is Fine" meme encapsulates the spirit of the IT profession. It's a badge of honor that says, "We've faced the fire, and we're still standing." Whether it's dealing with a catastrophic software failure, navigating the wild waters of remote work, or simply sharing a laugh during a tedious meeting, it reminds us that humor is an invaluable tool in our tech toolkit. As we continue to debug not just our code but also our daily lives, let's remember to keep the laughter alive because, in the end, it's the shared chuckles that make the chaos worthwhile.

The Meme War: A Battle of Wits

In the world of IT, a new battlefield has emerged, one where the weapons are memes and the ammunition is pure wit. This is the Meme War, a relentless struggle for supremacy in the digital age. Picture the scene: a team of developers huddled around their screens, not debugging code but crafting the perfect meme to ridicule their latest software update. The air is tense, punctuated by the occasional chuckle as one colleague unveils a meme that perfectly captures the existential dread of compiling code at 3 AM. These moments are not just distractions but the lifeblood of office camaraderie, turning mundane tasks into a vibrant spectacle of humor.

The war doesn't just rage in the confines of the office; it spills over into the wilds of social media, where IT professionals wage campaigns of hilarity. A particularly clever meme about the trials of remote work—complete with a dog that seems to be judging your every Zoom call—goes viral, earning likes and retweets aplenty. Each meme serves as a battle standard, a declaration of solidarity among those who understand the absurdities of tech life. It's a reminder that, despite the stress of deadlines and the chaos of endless updates, laughter is our most powerful tool, capable of turning the darkest moments of coding misadventures into relatable gold.

Yet, the Meme War is not without its casualties. In one infamous incident, a tech support team member inadvertently sparked a meme frenzy by sharing a screenshot of a particularly ridiculous support call. "Is there a way to turn off the internet? I keep getting pop-ups!" became the rallying cry for a week-long meme storm, with exaggerated images of tech support agents pulling their hair out. The sheer absurdity of the situation reminded everyone that while we may be experts in our field, we are not immune to the occasional brain freeze. This blend of expertise and humor keeps the IT trenches lively.

As the war escalates, so do the pranks. The office becomes a playground where memes come to life, with colleagues reenacting scenes from their favorite tech-related jokes. An unsuspecting coder replaces their chair with a whoopee cushion, triggering a chain reaction of laughter and a flurry of meme-worthy expressions. Each prank and meme serves as a reminder that while we are serious about our work, we are equally serious about our fun. The office transforms into a battlefield where laughter is the only currency, and the ability to craft a witty comeback can mean the difference between victory and defeat.

In the end, the Meme War is more than just a series of inside jokes; it's a testament to the resilience of the IT community. Humor is a vital release valve in a field often characterized by stress and technical jargon. Whether it's sharing a laugh over a poorly timed update or bonding over the latest meme that captures the trials of remote work, we find strength in our shared experiences. So, the next time you're knee-deep in code or trapped in a meeting that feels like a never-ending loop, remember: the Meme War is always winnable, one laugh at a time.

CHAPTER EIGHT

The Trials of Remote Work

Zoom Calls and Pajama Pants

In the brave new world of remote work, where the line between professional and comfortable attire has blurred to non-existent, Zoom calls have become the battleground for sartorial decisions. Just imagine: a team meeting, faces glowing in their tiny boxes, while the professional upper halves of participants are impeccably dressed in suits or blouses, a stark contrast to the pajama pants below. It's the ultimate test of multitasking—how to appear polished while secretly enjoying the comfort of your favorite flannel pants. After all, no one can see what's happening beneath the desk, right? Unless your cat makes a surprise appearance during your presentation, prompting you to stand up and reveal your questionable fashion choices to the entire team.

Then there are the countless Zoom mishaps that have left us all in stitches. One fateful afternoon, amid a serious discussion about project timelines, a colleague accidentally turned on a filter that transformed him into an animated potato. While the rest of us tried to focus on deadlines, he cheerfully embraced his new identity and began offering "spud-tacular" insights. It was a classic case of hilarity meeting professionalism as we all struggled to keep straight faces while discussing the urgency of a client presentation. Who knew that a potato could offer such valuable feedback? This little incident inspired a new office meme that circulated for weeks, bringing a light-heartedness to our usually dreary project updates.

As the meetings progressed, so did the creative ways that IT professionals entertained themselves during these video calls. One tech-savvy team decided to implement a "pajama day" during their weekly catch-up. The catch? You had to wear the most ridiculous pajama pants you could find. Suddenly, a rainbow unicorn pattern with a matching headband became the show's star. The competition was fierce, and by the end of the meeting, we had a parade of pajama-clad warriors showcasing their finest sleepwear. The camaraderie was palpable as we cheered each other on, proving that even in remote work, the spirit of office pranks and tech shenanigans can thrive.

Of course, not every Zoom call goes off without a hitch. There was a time when a colleague, oblivious to the fact that her camera was still on, decided to take a quick snack break. A masterclass in multitasking followed as she attempted to eat a giant sandwich while still engaging in the meeting. The visual of her struggling to maintain professionalism while grappling with her lunch was priceless. It was a moment that perfectly encapsulated the trials of remote work, reminding us that while we may be working from home, balancing work and personal life is as real as ever.

As we continue to navigate this new normal, embracing humor in our everyday tech interactions is essential. These moments have created a unique bond among IT professionals, from pajama pants to unexpected interruptions. We've learned to laugh at our mishaps, turning them into legendary tales that fuel our office culture, even if it's virtual. So, the next time you log into a Zoom call, remember to check your pants before you stand up, and never underestimate the power of a good laugh amid coding misadventures and tech support shenanigans. After all, humor is the ultimate debugging tool in the IT trenches.

The Great Wi-Fi Outage Of 2023

In 2023, a cataclysmic event shook the very foundations of the IT world: The Great Wi-Fi Outage. It all began on a seemingly normal Tuesday morning when the coffee machine was brewing, and the hope of a productive day filled with code and caffeine loomed bright. Little did we know, the Wi-Fi gods were conspiring against us. With the flick of a switch—or rather, the flick of a router—the signal vanished, leaving the office in chaos usually reserved for an IT conference where the Wi-Fi password mysteriously changes every hour.

As the news of the outage spread, panic ensued. The office was filled with frantic keyboard clacking as people attempted to connect to the most reliable source of the internet: their mobile data. But, of course, the looming specter of data overages haunted us like a bad coding error. In a desperate attempt to salvage the situation, Greg from accounting decided it was time to break out the old Ethernet cables. Watching him crawl under desks like a tech-savvy caterpillar was the highlight of my day. Who knew that a simple cable could turn a corporate environment into a scene reminiscent of a nature documentary?

While we were battling our inner demons over whether to join the Ethernet revolution, our boss, Tom, had a different plan. He gathered us for an impromptu meeting to "brainstorm solutions." We all knew this was code for "let's talk about how I have no idea what to do." As he scribbled nonsensical diagrams on the whiteboard, we couldn't help but stifle our laughter. One diagram resembled a Wi-Fi signal attempting to escape a black hole, while another looked suspiciously like a poorly drawn cat. This was the equivalent of a Shakespearean tragedy in the tech world, and we all played our roles beautifully.

Hours became an eternity as we resorted to the ancient art of face-to-face communication. Conversations flowed like the sweet nectar of connectivity, with people gathering around desks to share memes and stories of tech support calls gone wrong. Lisa from HR recounted the time she spent thirty minutes explaining to her grandmother how to turn on her Wi-Fi, only to realize it was still unplugged. The laughter echoed through the halls, morphing the outage into a bizarre team-building exercise where camaraderie replaced connectivity. Who knew that a lack of Wi-Fi could lead to such bonding experiences, more effective than any trust fall exercise?

As the sun began to set, we were left with one final twist: the outage was caused by a squirrel chewing through a cable outside. In true tech fashion, we couldn't help but create a meme to commemorate our furry foe. As we packed up our laptops and headed home that night, we felt a strange sense of unity. The Great Wi-Fi Outage of 2023 had turned into an unexpected adventure, filled with laughter, a touch of absurdity, and a reminder that sometimes, the best connections are the ones we take away from the screen. After all, the real fun begins when the Wi-Fi goes down in IT.

CHAPTER NINE

Funny IT Department Meetings

The Meeting That Should Have Been an Email

The conference room buzzed with the energy of a dozen IT professionals, each armed with laptops and an eagerness to discuss the latest update on the network switch that had gone rogue. As the clock ticked closer to the meeting's start time, the usual banter about the best memes from the latest tech conference faded into a collective sigh. Clearly, this gathering was destined to be a colossal waste of time, yet here we were, trapped in a room with a whiteboard covered in acronyms that even the most seasoned techies struggled to decipher. If only someone had the courage to send an email instead.

As the meeting commenced, our manager, Steve, launched into a detailed PowerPoint presentation that began with the words "network infrastructure" and devolved into tales of his cat, Mr. Whiskers, who had somehow managed to unplug the router while chasing a laser pointer. While some of us tried to hide our snickers behind our hands, others were openly rolling their eyes. Can you imagine the horror of Mr. Whiskers being the main topic of discussion when we could have been tackling actual issues? Half the room was mentally drafting an email to HR suggesting mandatory training on "How to Keep Personal Stories Out of Professional Meetings."

Just when we thought it couldn't get any worse, the projector decided to join the circus and started flickering like it was having a seizure. With each flash, it was as if the universe was trying to send us a message: "This meeting should have been an email." The IT department, masters of troubleshooting, couldn't even figure out how to reset the projector. Meanwhile, one brave soul in the back row attempted to take matters into his own hands by yelling, "Have you tried turning it off and on again?" Apparently, that advice was not just for tech support calls but also applicable to our sanity.

As the hour passed, we drifted into a collective daydream of what we could have accomplished in wasted time. Some envisioned finally fixing that pesky bug in the code that had haunted them for weeks, while others fantasized about playing video games or binge-watching that new sci-fi series they had heard so much about. One cheeky developer even scribbled a fake agenda on the whiteboard, listing "Discussing Office Pranks" and "Tech Shenanigans: A Deep Dive," which elicited a few snickers and a glimmer of hope that the meeting might take a turn for the ridiculous.

Finally, as we approached the two-hour mark, Steve wrapped up his presentation with a flourish and a request for questions. The silence was deafening, broken only by a single pen rolling off a table. We all knew what was coming next: a suggestion for a follow-up meeting to dive deeper into Mr. Whiskers' router escapades. As we filed out of the room, grumbling about the lost time, we made a pact never to let such a travesty occur again. The next time, we would take a stand, send that email, and save our meetings for the truly important—like deciding on the office lunch order or planning the next legendary office prank.

Rants and Riddles: The Meeting of the Mind

In the world of IT, where lines of code often blur reality, a peculiar phenomenon occurs when minds collide: the epic showdown of rants versus riddles. Picture this: a conference room filled with seasoned IT pros, each armed with their favorite rants about the latest software bugs or the eternal struggle against printer malfunctions. Suddenly, someone tosses a riddle into the mix. "What has keys but can't open locks?" The room falls silent, minds racing to solve the riddle while simultaneously prepping their next rant about the latest Windows update that crashed half the office.

As the rants escalate, so does the humor. One IT veteran, known for his dramatic flair, launches into a passionate tirade about client requests. "Why do they always want impossible things? I can't turn back time, folks! I'm an IT guy, not Doctor Who!" Laughter erupts, and as the riddle goes unanswered, someone chimes in, "A piano! But really, can it play 'My Heart Will Go On' while the server is down?" The situation's absurdity only fuels the fiery debate, transforming frustrations into a comedic contest of wit.

It's not just the rants that provide comic relief; the ridiculous tech support calls inevitably surface during these gatherings. One brave soul recalls a call about a user who couldn't connect to Wi-Fi. "Turns out she was trying to connect her toaster!" The room erupts into hysterics. Riddles about connectivity follow, and someone quips, "What do you call a Wi-Fi connection in the bathroom? A loo-tube!" The laughter serves as a reminder that even in tech trenches, absurdity reigns supreme.

As the meeting progresses, the riddle-rant dichotomy evolves into a playful competition. Participants throw out absurd tech-related riddles, each more ridiculous than the last. "Why was the computer cold?" "Because it left its Windows open!" The rants morph into a series of witty comebacks, each IT professional trying to outdo the other. The atmosphere transforms from mundane to electric, with the shared humor bridging the gaps caused by endless coding hours and remote work fatigue.

By the end of the meeting, something remarkable happens: grievances dissolve under layers of laughter. The rants that once seemed burdensome become stories everyone can relate to, while the riddles are delightful distractions from the daily grind. As everyone leaves the room, they carry a sense of camaraderie and a renewed appreciation for the lighter side of their tech-laden lives. The meeting of minds—rants and riddles alike—reminds them that humor is the best debugging tool they have in the world of IT.

CHAPTER TEN

Techie Pet Peeves

The Overuse of Buzzwords

In the fast-paced world of IT, buzzwords are like the glitter in a toddler's craft project — flashy, everywhere, and often completely unnecessary. You can hardly attend a meeting without hearing someone drop terms like "synergy," "disruption," or "pivot" as if they were the Holy Grail of communication. It's as if we've collectively agreed that the more obscure the term, the smarter we sound. But let's be honest, nobody knows what "disruptive innovation" means, yet it gets thrown around more than the last slice of pizza at a late-night coding session.

Consider the infamous IT conference, where a parade of speakers attempts to out-buzzword each other like it's an Olympic sport. You've got the keynote speaker who starts with, "Let's circle back to our core competencies," you can practically hear the audience's collective groan. Meanwhile, in the back of the room, a brave soul attempts to track how often "game-changer" is mentioned, only to end up with a headache and a new side hustle as a professional buzzword counter. If only we could harness the energy from all those eye rolls, we might finally have enough power to run the coffee machine without a glitch.

In tech support, buzzwords take on a life of their own. Imagine this: a panicked user calls in, their computer is on the fritz, and instead of a straightforward explanation, the IT professional responds with, "Let's leverage our resources to optimize your user experience." The user wonders if they just called for tech support or accidentally dialed into a motivational seminar. Moments like these make you wonder if we should drop the jargon and have a straightforward conversation. "Your computer is broken. Let's fix it." But then again, where's the fun in that?

In reality, buzzwords can often lead to some of the best office pranks. You've got the classic "buzzword bingo" game, where the winner gets to call out "synergy" at the most inappropriate moment in a meeting. Or how about when someone set up a fake email chain with jargon-laden phrases and sent it to the entire department? The ensuing confusion was so entertaining that it became an impromptu lunch discussion about who could use the most ridiculous buzzwords in a single sentence. Spoiler alert: the record was broken when someone combined "paradigm shift" and "thought leader" in a single breath.

While buzzwords may be the bane of our existence, they also provide endless comedic material. The next time you find yourself rolling your eyes at yet another meeting filled with jargon, remember that you're not alone. In the IT trenches, we're all trying to decode the mystery of corporate speak while stifling laughter at the absurdity of it all. So, let's embrace the buzzwords, but just this once, let's do it with a wink and a nod because, at the end of the day, laughter is our best debugging tool.

When "Urgent" Becomes a Joke

In the high-stakes world of IT, the word "urgent" is tossed around more than a rubber chicken at a clown convention. One day, a panic-stricken manager stormed into our office, waving a laptop like it was on fire. "The client needs this fixed immediately!" they yelled, eyes wide and wild. We gathered around the screen, ready to solve the crisis, only to discover that the "urgent" problem was a typo in an email. The client desperately needed a quick fix because their latest newsletter referred to "bear markets" instead of "bare markets." Imagine the confusion at their next investment seminar—thankfully, we saved them from multiple awkward conversations about bears in business suits.

Then there was the time when our team was called to address a server outage that sent everyone into a tizzy. The urgency level reached DEFCON 1 as we scrambled to reach the issue's root. After three hours of diagnostics, we discovered that the server wasn't down at all; it was unplugged. We all shared a collective eye-roll, but the real kicker was when we learned that the intern had been using the server room as a personal charging station for his phone. It's hard to take "urgent" seriously when the biggest crisis of the day was an intern's need to keep his TikTok account alive.

Of course, no IT story is complete without tech support calls that redefine urgency. One memorable call came in from a user who was convinced that their computer was possessed. As we dug deeper into the issue, the user revealed that their screen was flickering and making strange noises. After a few minutes of questioning, it turned out that the "ghostly" flickering was just an old screen trying to keep up with the latest Windows updates. We assured them their computer wasn't haunted, but they were still convinced it was a case of "The Exorcist: Silicon Edition." I can only imagine how they explained that to their friends at the bar.

Let's not forget those awkward moments during tech conferences when the urgency of showcasing the latest software turns into a complete circus act. Picture this: a well-prepared presenter stands in front of a packed audience, only for their demo to crash spectacularly in front of everyone. Desperate to salvage their dignity, they start cracking jokes about the "unexpected downtime" being a part of the new "feature." The audience isn't laughing with them; they're laughing at them, and soon it feels like a stand-up routine gone wrong. At that moment, "urgent" becomes a punchline, and the presenter learns that sometimes, the best software is a healthy dose of humility.

As we navigate the absurdities of IT, we realize that when "urgent" becomes a joke, it's often the best way to cope with the chaos surrounding us. We bond over shared laughter during meetings filled with techie pet peeves and the occasional meme that comes to life. Whether a coding misadventure or a remote work disaster, humor is the ultimate debugging tool. So the next time someone shouts "urgent" in the office, remember: it might be the perfect setup for a punchline rather than a crisis, and who doesn't love a good laugh amidst the madness of IT?

CHAPTER ELEVEN

Parody of Popular Software and Tools

The Misadventures of "Bugzilla"

In the bustling world of software development, few names evoke as much laughter and eye-rolling as "Bugzilla." For the uninitiated, Bugzilla is a bug-tracking system that has become a rite of passage for many developers. However, to those who have had the misfortune of using it, Bugzilla is a labyrinthine maze of confusion, where finding a bug is often harder than squashing it. One fateful Friday afternoon, a team of developers decided to engage in an epic quest to conquer the mystical beast that was Bugzilla, armed with nothing but their wits and an overabundance of caffeine.

As the team gathered around their monitors, they quickly realized that Bugzilla had taken on a life of its own. Each click felt like a dice roll in a game of chance. The first developer, eager to log a simple bug, typed in the details only to be greeted with a cryptic error message that seemed to be written in an ancient language. The message read, "File not found. Or maybe it is. Who knows?" Cue the chorus of laughter as the developers began to speculate wildly about the possible location of this elusive file, with theories ranging from a parallel universe to a vacation in the Bermuda Triangle.

With spirits high, the team decided to play a round of "Bug Roulette," where they would randomly select an existing bug to investigate. The chosen bug, labeled "Feature Request: Make the Interface More User-Friendly," was a cruel joke. The interface was so user-unfriendly that one team member likened it to trying to solve a Rubik's Cube blindfolded. They spent the next hour attempting to decipher the unintuitive layout; each taking turns reading the documentation, which was so outdated it could have been an entry in a history textbook. It was a contest of who could come up with the most absurd suggestion to "improve" the user experience, from adding animated unicorns to making the entire interface accessible only via interpretive dance.

As the afternoon wore on, the team decided to spice things up by pranking their unsuspecting colleague, Steve, who had just joined the team and was blissfully unaware of Bugzilla's notorious reputation. They concocted an elaborate story about a hidden feature that allowed users to communicate directly with the Bugzilla developers through a secret "whisper" function. Steve, ever the eager beaver, spent a good hour trying to find this mythical option, only to be met with uproarious laughter when they finally revealed the prank. His bewildered expression was priceless, as if he had just been told that the sky was actually green.

The day culminated in a conference call with their project manager, oblivious to their earlier antics. As the team tried to explain the bugs they had encountered while using Bugzilla, they could barely contain their laughter. The project manager, clearly confused, kept asking for clarifications, misinterpreting their jokes as serious issues. Ultimately, they all agreed that while Bugzilla might be the bane of their existence, it was also the source of some of their best laughs. After all, in the ever-serious world of IT, sometimes the most effective debugging tool is a healthy dose of humor and camaraderie.

"Excel-erating" Through Life's Problems

In the grand saga of IT life, problems often loom like a pop-up window at the most inconvenient moment. Picture this: you're knee-deep in code, trying to figure out why your new feature is throwing errors like a toddler throwing tantrums. Each keystroke feels like a gamble, and when you think you've nailed it, you hear the dreaded words, "Have you tried turning it off and on again?" It's a universal truth in tech support that the simplest solutions often come from those who haven't spent the last eight hours wrestling with the complexities of your code. The irony is that you sometimes wish to turn off your brain and reboot your sanity.

Speaking of sanity, let's talk about the office shenanigans that keep us from losing our minds entirely. You know it's been a long week when the highlight of your day is watching your coworker attempt to explain the intricacies of JavaScript to the intern, who's still trying to figure out how to connect to Wi-Fi. Cue the classic "I'm just going to Google it" moment, which inevitably leads to a 30-minute digression into the depths of conspiracy theories about why the office printer only works on Thursdays. When the printer jams, it's not just a technical issue; it's a team-building exercise as everyone gathers around, offering unsolicited advice while trying to decipher the cryptic error message that looks more like an ancient hieroglyph than a tech problem.

Then there are those tech support calls that could easily be mistaken for comedy sketches. You've got the user who insists they didn't change anything, yet their desktop wallpaper now features a cat riding a unicorn. Or the one who calls in a panic because their laptop has "disappeared," only to find out they left it on the roof of their car during their morning commute. Now, you can't help but wonder if these mishaps are a part of some cosmic joke aimed at IT professionals. The universe is conspiring to keep you on your toes, ensuring you'll have a story worth telling at the next conference— preferably over a pint of beer.

And let's not ignore the joy of remote work, where the trials and tribulations take on a whole new dimension. There's the Zoom meeting where someone forgets to mute their mic. At the same time, their dog holds an impromptu barking competition, and the inevitable "Can you see my screen?" somehow becomes a group therapy session as everyone realizes they've all been staring at the same "buffering" icon for ten minutes. The real kicker is when the meeting ends, and you breathe a sigh of relief, only to find out the chat was filled with memes poking fun at your "technical difficulties." It's a reminder that no matter how frustrating tech issues can be, you're never alone in this digital wilderness.

Through all these hilarious misadventures, the takeaway is clear: life in the IT trenches is best navigated with a hearty laugh. Whether dealing with unexpected tech fails or the absurdities of office life, humor is the secret weapon that transforms chaos into camaraderie. So the next time you find yourself face-to-face with an insurmountable problem, remember to embrace the absurdity. After all, in a world filled with error messages and quirky user behavior, sometimes the best solution is to laugh it off and keep "Excel-erating" through life's delightful disasters.

CHAPTER TWELVE

Conclusion: Laughing Through the Code

Finding Humor in the Chaos

In the whirlwind of deadlines, bug fixes, and endless meetings, IT professionals often find themselves in situations that could easily qualify as comic relief. Take, for example, the classic scenario of a tech support call where the user has accidentally unplugged their computer. The conversation typically starts with the user panicking, convinced their entire digital life has vanished. "I can't find my files!" they wail, oblivious that their monitor is dark because they've pulled the plug. This moment highlights that no matter how advanced technology becomes, a little humor goes a long way in diffusing the stress of the situation. After all, nothing says "I love my job," quite like explaining to someone how to reconnect their power cord while suppressing a chuckle.

Office pranks are another cherished tradition in the IT world, where we wield our keyboards like the finest instruments of chaos. There's nothing quite like the satisfaction of swapping a colleague's desktop wallpaper with a photo of a cat dressed as a tech support agent, complete with oversized glasses and a headset. The ensuing confusion is priceless when they return from lunch to a feline overlord staring back at them. Such harmless pranks serve as a reminder that amid the high-stakes environment of coding and debugging, a little levity can help maintain camaraderie and keep morale high. Plus, it's a great way to bond over shared laughter when the inevitable "Who did this?" question fills the air.

Then there are misadventures during coding sessions, which often resemble a slapstick comedy more than a serious endeavor. Picture a programmer who accidentally deletes the entire database instead in an effort to implement a new feature. As they frantically try to restore it, they can't help but recall the moment their coffee cup tipped over, cascading its contents onto the keyboard. These moments remind us that even the most skilled among us can have a day where everything goes wrong, and laughter is the best medicine when faced with a digital disaster. After all, if you're going to crash and burn, you might as well do it with a sense of humor.

With their endless sessions and networking opportunities, IT conferences also provide a goldmine of comedic material. Imagine the tech guru who confidently presents his innovative new app, only for it to crash spectacularly on stage. The awkward silence that follows, punctuated only by the sound of his heart shattering, is enough to make anyone squirm. Yet, instead of sinking into despair, he turns to the audience and quips, "Well, at least you know it's not just you!" This ability to laugh at oneself in the face of failure creates a more relaxed atmosphere and fosters an environment where creativity and innovation can flourish. After all, if you can't laugh at your own tech blunders, are you really living the IT dream?

Finding humor in the chaos has never been more vital in remote work. With colleagues popping in and out of video calls in various states of attire—some in business on top and pajamas on the bottom—it's a veritable circus. The classic "Can you hear me?" followed by a muted mic and frantic gestures has become a ritual that transcends company lines. Each awkward moment, from pets interrupting meetings to unexpected background noises, creates an endless supply of material for office memes. As we navigate this new normal, embracing the absurdities of remote work helps cultivate resilience and camaraderie, proving that even in our most chaotic moments, we can find laughter amidst the pixels.

The Future of IT: A Comedy of Errors

In the ever-evolving realm of IT, where technology changes faster than a programmer can say, "It works on my machine," the future promises to be a comedy of errors that even the best stand-up comedians would struggle to script. Picture this: a new software update rolls out, and suddenly your state-of-the-art office printer thinks it's a coffee maker and starts brewing a fresh pot instead of printing the quarterly reports. As everyone gathers around, cups in hand, the IT department scrambles to explain to management that they got the "print" and "brew" commands mixed up… again. It's a classic case of miscommunication that leaves everyone caffeinated and questions the sanity of all involved.

Meanwhile, as remote work continues to be the norm, the future of IT is riddled with its own set of laughable disasters. Imagine a virtual meeting where the entire team is debating the latest tech stack, only for one poor soul to realize they've been sharing their screen, revealing a series of cat memes that, let's be honest, are way more entertaining than the actual agenda. As colleagues try to stifle their laughter, the host, blissfully unaware of the spectacle, drones on about cloud migration while everyone else wonders how to get a copy of that meme for their next office prank. Clearly, the future isn't just about bytes and bandwidth; it's also about bytes of humor shared across digital platforms.

And then there are the tech support calls destined to become legendary. One brave IT professional takes a call from a user who is convinced the new AI bot is plotting against them. "It keeps suggesting I buy printer ink!" they exclaim their voice a mix of panic and disbelief. After a long conversation with tech jargon and attempted reassurance, the IT pro finally asks the user to check if the bot is connected to the Wi-Fi. "Oh, it's not?" the user replies, "Does that mean it's just a really smart toaster?" At this point, the line goes quiet as the IT professional tries to stifle their laughter, realizing they have created a new meme about toaster supremacy in the digital age.

IT conferences will be a treasure trove of hilarity as we look toward the future. Imagine a panel discussion on the next big thing in cybersecurity, only for the keynote speaker to accidentally log into their personal email instead of the conference platform, revealing a string of messages from their mom asking why they haven't found a nice girlfriend yet. The audience erupts into laughter, and suddenly, the talk shifts from firewalls to dating apps as everyone starts brainstorming the perfect tech-themed pick-up lines. "Are you a bug? Because you're making my system crash!" becomes the unofficial tagline of the conference, proving that even in the most serious of fields, humor can bridge the gap between techies and their more social aspirations.

In this delightful landscape of tech mishaps and blunders, the future of IT is not just about solving problems but also about embracing the laughter that comes with the territory. From coding misadventures that leave developers scratching their heads to office pranks that could rival any sitcom plot, the IT world is a playground of comedic potential. As we navigate this unpredictable terrain, we must remember to keep our sense of humor intact, for it is our greatest asset in a field where chaos often reigns supreme. After all, if we can't laugh at our own missteps, we might end up being the punchline in someone else's story.

www.ingramcontent.com/pod-product-compliance
Lightning Source LLC
Chambersburg PA
CBHW071031050326
40689CB00014B/3611